PRACTICAL APPROACH OF MACHINE TRANSLATION TO BUILD INTELEGENT TRANSLATOR

Translation of Global Language English to Indian Ancient Language Sanskrit.

Prof S.P Godse

Prof S.S. Godse

Seattle Digital Publications, India

DEDICATION

"This book is Dedicated to my Great **A**ai & **P**apa, **"Pramodini and Pandurang"** without Them, I would be nothing."

ABOUT AUTHOR

Prof S.P Godse has obtained his B.E degree in computer engineering from AVCOE, Savitribai Phule Pune University, Pune, India and M.E. degree in computer Science and engineering from SCOE, Savitribai Phule Pune University, Pune India. His Areas of interest are **Vehicular Adhoc Network, Mobile Adhoc Network, Natural Language Processing, and Object-Oriented Programming, Object Oriented Modeling, Software Engineering. he has Authored 4 books on subject like: Embedded system and Internet of thing, Software testing and Quality Assurance.** he has published more than 25 papers in international and national journals and conferences. currently he is pursuing his PH. D in computer engineering from Smt. Kashibai Navale College of engineering, SPPU, Pune, India

Prof. S. S Godse has obtained her B.E. degree in E&TC engineering from NDMVP, Savitribai Phule Pune University, Pune, India and M.E in E&TC (Signal Processing) from MKSSS's Cummins college of engineering for women, Pune, Savitribai Phule Pune University, Pune, India. Her areas of interest are **Mobile Adhoc network. she has Published more than 20 papers in international and national Journals and conferences.** currently she is working as professor in Vishwakarma University, Pune, India

Technical Reviewer

 **Prof. Ashish P. Ramdasi** was born in Osmanabad, Maharashtra, India in 1986. He received the **B.E. degree in Computer Science and Engineering from B.A.M.U. university Aurangabad**, India and **M.Tech from J.N.T.U. Hyderabad ,India**. He is research Scholar at **H.I.T.S. Chennai, India**. His current research interest includes **Data Mining, Text Mining, Information Retrieval, Machine Learning**. He has been with **the** department of Computer Engineering, Sinhgad Academy of Engineering, Pune, where he is working as an **Assistant Professor**. He has 8 years of experience in teaching.

He has published more **than 20 papers in National/International journals** and has participated in conferences to enhance the knowledge of a specific domain. He is also a **Co-author** of "**How to Learn Python in 100 Minutes**" book, available on **Amazon.in**. He was coordinator of more than 10 workshops of different domains. Being a coordinator of **IIT Bombay Spoken Tutorial,** He has got the opportunity to enhance the knowledge of students through arranging different language courses. He has teaching expertise in **Data Structure, Digital Electronics, Object Oriented Programming, Computer Security and Data Mining**.

Area focused in this book is very emerging area of research. Translation of text is become essential need of many tech-savvy applications like **mobile phones, web portal, embedded device** etc.   This book addresses thorough **knowledge of translation process**. It explained practical example of English to Sanskrit translation. Author has also given future **scope of translation mechanism for developing a new English to regional language translation tool**. This book also contains discovery of knowledge of translation domain with example. **It was amazing experience of reading this book.**

CONTENTS

Chapter 1
INTRODUCTION

INTRODUCTION

Translation is one of the need of global society for communicating thought, ideas of one country with the other. Translation is the process of interpretation of text meaning and subsequent production of equivalent text also called as communicating the same meaning (message) in another language.

A human translator is not easily available or very rare and inaccessible to common man. Machine translation is the domain of Natural language processing and the area of AI. AI is very useful in providing the people with a machine, which understand and divert the language from one language to another.

English to Sanskrit machine translation is based on machine translation using NLP. Here bilingual translation is considered. Source language for translation is English and destination language is the Sanskrit language. Translation of languages required knowledge of the source and target language grammar, vocabulary and symbols.

1.1 ORIGIN OF THE PROBLEM

Work in the area of Machine Translation has been going on for several decades and it was only during the early 90s that a promising translation technology began to emerge with advanced researches in the field of Artificial Intelligence and Computational Linguistics. This held the promise of successfully developing usable Machine Translation Systems in certain well-defined domains. India, being a multilingual and multicultural country with a population of approximately 950 million people and 18 constitutionally recognized languages, needs a translation system for instant transfer of information and knowledge.

Another motivation for taking up this challenge is that English is a global business language used all over the world for business. But in India very few people are able to understand English to overcome this we required translator which will convert English into the native language. In India, Sanskrit is an ancient language almost all of the Indian language derived from the Sanskrit language so it acts as an Interlingua for translation to and from Indian languages.

1.2 KNOWLEDGE REQUIRED FOR TRANSLATION

Translation of languages required Knowledge of source language, knowledge of target language, knowledge of various correspondences between the source language and target language.

- **Distinguish Several Kinds of Linguistic knowledge:**
1. **Morphological Knowledge:** knowledge about how words can be constructed.
2. **Syntactic Knowledge:** Knowledge of how sentences and other sorts of phrases can be made up out of words.
3. **Semantic Knowledge:** Knowledge about what words and phrases mean, about how the meaning of a phrase is related to the meaning of its component words.
- **Representing Linguistic Knowledge:** In general, syntax is concerned with two slightly different sorts of analysis of sentences.
1. **Constituent or phrase structure analysis:** division of sentence into their constituent parts and the categorization of these parts as nominal, verbal and so on.
2. **Grammar relation:** the assignment of grammatical relation such as Subject, Object, Head and so on to various part of the sentence.
- **Grammar and constituent structure:** Sentences are made up of words, traditionally categorized into part of speech or categories including nouns, verbs, adjectives, adverbs & prepositions.
A Grammar of a language is a set of rules which says how these parts of speech can be put together to make grammatical or well-formed sentences.

1.3 FOCUS OF TRANSLATOR DEVELOPED BY AUTHOR

1. Translator explain in this book is providing the tool for converting English sentence into Sanskrit sentence.
2. It provides functionality for Tokenization, Part of speech tagging, Parsing and separation of compound sentences into simple sentences.
3. Major efforts are required for the creation of databases, bilingual dictionary.
4. Designing of grammar rules which we are using for the formation of source and destination language parse tree.
5. Context-based sentence translation is one of the latest features added into translator.
6. If the translation is not available nearest matching is provided for given sentence.

1.4 FUNCTIONALITY AND APPLICABILITY

English to Sanskrit machine translation is purely research topic which is designed using natural language processing approach.

Functionality Provided
1.   Accept the source text in English from the user.
2.   Separate the token from a sentence by Tokenization.
3.   Part of speech tagging.
4.   Forming the parse tree of source sentence.
5.   Forming the parse tree of Target sentence.
6.   Extraction of the meaning of English words from the bilingual dictionary.
7.   Translation of sentence in to Sanskrit sentence.

1.5 SUMMARY

This chapter gives an introduction of application which I implemented; a contribution of the application is listed. Basic knowledge required for translation is explained in short.

CHAPTER 2
SURVEY ON MACHINE

2.1 HISTORY OF MACHINE TRANSLATION

The translation of natural languages by machine, first dreamt of in the seventeenth century, has become a reality in the late twentieth. Computer programs are producing translations - not perfect translations, for that is an ideal to which no human translator can aspire; nor translations of literary texts, for the subtleties and nuances of poetry are beyond computational analysis; but translations of technical manuals, scientific documents, commercial prospectuses, administrative memoranda, medical reports. Machine translation is not primarily an area of abstract intellectual inquiry but the application of computer and language sciences to the development of systems answering practical needs. After an outline of basic features, the history of machine translation is traced from the pioneers and early systems of the 1950s and 1960s, the impact of the ALPAC report in the mid-1960s, the revival in the 1970s, the appearance of commercial and operational systems in the 1980s, research during the 1980s, new developments in research in the 1990s, and the growing use of systems in the past decade. This brief history can mention only the major and most significant systems and projects.

2.2 BASIC FEATURE AND TERMINOLOGY

The term 'machine translation' (MT) refers to computerized systems responsible for the production of translations with or without human assistance. It excludes computer-based translation tools which support translators by providing access to online dictionaries, remote terminology databanks, transmission and reception of texts, etc. The boundaries between machine-aided human translation (MAHT) and human aided machine translation (HAMT) are often uncertain and the term computer-aided translation (CAT) can cover both, but the central core of MT itself is the automation of the full translation process. Although the ideal goal of MT systems to produce a high-quality translation, in practice the output is usually revised (post-edited). It should be noted that in this respect MT does not differ from the output of most human translators which is normally revised by a second translator before dissemination. However, the types of errors produced by MT systems do differ from those of human translators (incorrect prepositions, articles, pronouns, verb tenses, etc.). Post-editing is the norm, but in certain circumstances, MT output may be unedited or only lightly revised, e.g. if it is intended only for specialists familiar with the text subject. The output might also serve as a rough draft for a human translator, i.e. as a 'pre-translation'.

The translation quality of MT systems may be improved either, most obviously, by developing more sophisticated methods or by imposing certain restrictions on the input. The system may be designed, for example, to deal with texts limited to the sublanguage (vocabulary and grammar) of a particular subject field (e.g. biochemistry) and/or document type (e.g. patents). Alternatively, input texts may be written in a controlled language, which restricts the range of vocabulary and avoids homonymy and complex sentence structures. A third option is to require input texts to be marked (pre-edited) with indicators of prefixes, suffixes, word divisions, phrase and clause boundaries, or of different grammatical categories (e.g. the noun convict and its homonymous verb convict). Finally, the system itself may refer to problems of ambiguity and selection to human operators (usually translators) for resolution during the processes of translation itself, in an interactive mode.

Systems are designed either for two particular languages (bilingual systems) or for more than a single pair of languages (multilingual systems). Bilingual systems may be designed to operate either in only one direction (unidirectional), e.g. from Japanese into English, or in both directions (bidirectional).

Multilingual systems are usually intended to be bidirectional; most bilingual systems are unidirectional. In overall system design, there have been three basic types. The first (and historically oldest) type is generally referred to as the **'Direct Translation'** approach: the MT system is designed in all details specifically for one particular pair of languages, e.g. Russian as the language of the original texts, the source language, and English as the language of the translated texts, the target language. Translation is direct from the source language (SL) text to the target language (TL) text; the basic assumption is that the vocabulary and syntax of SL texts need not be analyzed any more than strictly necessary for the resolution of ambiguities, the correct identification of TL expressions and the specification of TL word order; in other words, SL analysis is oriented specifically to one particular TL. Typically, systems consist of a large bilingual dictionary and a single monolithic program for analyzing and generating texts; such 'direct translation' systems are necessarily bilingual and unidirectional.

The second basic design strategy is the **'Interlingua'** approach, which assumes that it is possible to convert SL texts into representations common to more than one language. From such interlingual representations, texts are generated in other languages. Translation is thus in two stages: from SL to the Interlingua (IL) and from the IL to the TL. Procedures for SL analysis are intended to be SL-specific and not oriented to any particular TL; likewise, programs for TL synthesis are TL-specific and not designed for input from particular SLs. A common argument for the Interlingua approach is economy of effort in a multilingual environment. Translation from and into n languages requires n (n-1) bilingual 'direct translation' systems, but with translation, via an Interlingua, just 2n interlingual programs are needed. With more than three languages the Interlingua approach is claimed to be more economical. On the other hand, the complexity of the Interlingua itself is greatly increased. Interlinguas may be based on an artificial language, an auxiliary language such as Esperanto, a set of semantic primitives presumed common to many or all languages, or a 'universal' language-independent vocabulary.

The third basic strategy is the less ambitious **'Transfer approach'**. Rather than operating in two stages through a single interlingual representation, there are three stages involving underlying (abstract) representations for both SL and TL texts. The first stage converts SL texts into abstract SL-oriented representations; the second stage converts these into equivalent TL-oriented representations, and the third generates the final TL texts. Whereas the Interlingua approach necessarily requires complete resolution of all ambiguities in the SL text so that translation into any other language is possible, in the transfer approach only those ambiguities inherent in the language in question are tackled; problems of lexical differences between languages are dealt with in the second stage (transfer proper). Transfer systems consist typically of three types of dictionaries (SL dictionary containing detailed morphological, grammatical and semantic information, similar TL dictionary, and a bilingual dictionary relating base SL forms and base TL forms) and various grammars (for SL analysis, TL synthesis and for the transformation of SL structures into TL forms).

Within the stages of analysis and synthesis (or generation), many MT systems exhibit clearly separated components involving different levels of linguistic description: morphology, syntax, and semantics. Hence, analysis may be divided into morphological analysis (identification of word endings, word compounds), syntactic analysis (identification of phrase structures, dependency, subordination, etc.), semantic analysis (resolution of lexical and structural ambiguities); synthesis may likewise pass through semantic synthesis (selection of appropriate compatible lexical and structural forms), syntactic synthesis (generation of required phrase and sentence structures), and morphological synthesis (generation of correct word forms). In transfer systems, the transfer component may also have separate programs dealing with the lexical transfer (selection of vocabulary equivalents) and with the structural transfer (transformation into TL-appropriate structures). In some earlier forms of transfer systems analysis did not involve a semantic stage; transfer was restricted to the conversion of syntactic structures, i.e. syntactic transfer alone.

In many older systems, particularly those of the 'direct translation' type the components of analysis; transfer and synthesis were not always clearly separated. Some of them also mixed data (dictionary and grammar) and processing rules and routines. Later systems have exhibited various degrees of modularity, so that system components, data, and programs can be adapted and changed without damage to overall system efficiency. A further stage in some recent systems is the reversibility of analysis and synthesis components, i.e. the data and transformations used in the analysis of a particular language are applied in reverse when generating texts in that language.

The direct translation approach was typical of the "first generation" of MT systems. The indirect approach of Interlingua and transfer based systems are often seen to characterize the "second generation" of MT system types. Both are based essentially on the specification of rules (for morphology, syntax, lexical selection, semantic analysis, and generation). Most recently, corpus-based methods have changed the traditional picture (see below). During the last five years, there is beginning to emerge as a "third generation" of hybrid systems combining the rule-based approaches of the earlier types and the more recent corpus-based methods. The differences between direct and indirect transfer and Interlingua, rule based, knowledge-based and corpus-based are becoming less useful for the categorization of systems. Transfer systems incorporate interlingual features (for certain areas of vocabulary and syntax); Interlingua systems include transfer components; rule-based systems make increasing use of probabilistic data and stochastic methods; statistics- and example-based systems include traditional rule-based grammatical categories and features; and so forth. These recent developments underline what has always been true, namely that MT research and MT systems adopt a variety of methodologies in order to tackle the full range of language phenomena, complexities of terminology and structure, misspellings, 'ungrammatical' sentences, neologisms, etc. The development of an operational MT system is necessarily a long-term 'engineering' task applying techniques which are well known, reliable and well tested.

2.3 SUMMARY

This chapter provides brief history of machine translation. It also includes the survey on day by day changes in the applicability of machine translation and features of translation.

CHAPTER 3
APPROACHES TO MACHINE TRANSLATION

Different approaches are available for performing machine translation. Research is going on improvement in available approaches and finding of new approaches for machine translation. In this chapter, I gave an example of some approaches which used for machine translation. I also explained approach which I am using for English to Sanskrit machine translation.

3.1 EXAMPLES OF TRADITIONAL MACHINE TRANSLATION

In its pure form, the statistics-based approach to MT makes use of no traditional linguistic data. The essence of the method is first to align phrases, word groups, and individual words of the parallel texts, and then to calculate the *probabilities* that any one word in a sentence of one language corresponds to a word or words in the translated sentence with which it is aligned in the other language. An essential feature is the availability of a suitable large bilingual corpus of reliable (authoritative) translations. This approach is often seen as 'anti-linguistics' and is most closely associated with the IBM research group at Yorktown Heights, NY (Brown et al. 1990), who had some success with non-linguistic approaches to speech recognition, and turned their attention to MT in the early 1990's. As already mentioned, the idea is to *model* the translation process in terms of statistical probabilities:

3.1.2 MT USING MULTIPLE TRANSLATION ENGINE AND SENTENCE PARTITIONING:

In this case, the source text is passed through a number of different MT systems, each using different techniques. One may be essentially lexicon based, another rule-based analysis and generation, a third example based or more purely statistical. In each case, built into the system will be a kind of scoring mechanism, by which the engine is able to evaluate for itself its 'confidence' in the output. For example, a rule-based engine may be able to reflect how sure it is of having been able to choose correctly between competing analyses. At the other end of the process is a kind of 'moderator' which will take the outputs of the various engines and compare them, choosing the highest scoring proposal, or confirm similar translations proposed by different engines, or perhaps even consolidating them by combining the best bits of each.

3.1.3 EXAMPLE BASED ENGLISH TO SANSKRIT MACHINE TRANSLATION: -

The Example Based Machine Translation (EBMT) is one of the most popular machine translation mechanisms which retrieve similar examples with their translation from the example database and adapting the examples to translate a new source text. It called the method "Translation by Analogy". The basic units of EBMT are sequences of words (phrases) and the basic techniques are the matching of input sentence (or phrases) with source example; phrase from the data base and the extraction of corresponding phrase from the database and the extraction of corresponding translation (translation phrase) and the "recombination" of the phrases as acceptable translation sentences. It is defined on the basis of data used in the translation process, and it is not enough to say that EBMT is "data driven" in contrast to "theory-driven" RBMT and that EBMT is "symbolic" in contrast to "non-symbolic" SMT.

3.1.4 DATA ORIENTED PARSING TECHNIQUE IN ENGLISH TO CHINESE MACHINE TRANSLATION:

Assuming human language perception and production depend on concrete past language experiences rather than on abstract grammar rules. By applying data oriented parsing technique for source language analysis procedure and same technique in target generation procedure and establish Data oriented procedure-based target generation mechanism.

3.1.5 HYBRID APPROACHES FOR MACHINE TRANSLATION:

Neither the example-based nor the statistics-based approaches to MT have turned out to be demonstrably better than the rule-based approaches, though each has shown some promise in certain cases. As a result of this, a number of **hybrid approaches** quickly emerged. Recognizing that some specific problems were particularly suited to an example-based approach, in some systems, there is an example-based component which is activated specifically to deal with the kinds of problems that is difficult to capture in a rule-based approach. Other hybrid systems combine rule-based analysis and generation with an example-based transfer. A third combination seems particularly suited to the thorny problem of spoken language translation, where for example elements of the analysis part may rely more heavily on statistical analysis, while transfer and generation are more suited to a rule-based approach.

3.2.1 TYPES OF RULE BASED APPROACH

1. Transfer based Machine Translation:

This type of machine translation based on the idea of Interlingua and is currently one of the most widely used areas. It is necessary to have an intermediate representation that captures the "meaning" of the original sentence in order to generate the correct translation.

2. Dictionary based Machine Translation:

A word is translated as a dictionary lookup may be done with or without morphological analysis.

3. Interlingua based Machine Translation:

In this intermediate representation must be independent of languages in question. whereas in transfer-based MT; it has some dependence on the language pair involved.

3.2.2 TYPE USED IN THIS PROJECT FROM RULE BASED APPROACH

Translator explained in this book uses Transfer based machine translation for English to Sanskrit machine translation.

Source and destination languages differ by syntax, by grammar, by the structure with each other. One strategy for doing MT is to translate by a process of overcoming these differences, altering the structure of input to make it conform to the rules of the target language.

This can be done by applying contrastive knowledge. That is knowledge about the differences between the two languages. A system based on this sometimes said to be based on the transfer model. Since transfer only results in a structure for the target language, it must be followed by the generation phase to actually create the output sentence.

So, the MT on this model requires three phases

1)   Analysis
2)   Transfer
3)   Generation.

3.2.3 TRANSFER ARCHITECTURE FOR MACHINE TRANSLATION

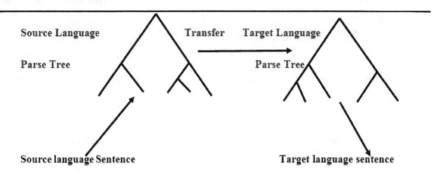

2.4 Syntax Transformation

If there is a syntactic difference between the source and target languages for e.g. English and French languages that differences are removed by reordering the syntax.

ENGLISH: - adjective preceding nouns.

FRENCH: - adjective follows the noun.

Temporarily postponing the question of how to translate the words. Let's consider how an MT system can overcome such differences

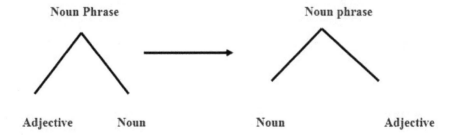

Fig. 3.2 A Simple Transformation that reorders adjective and nouns.

Here we transform one parse tree, suitable for describing in an English phrase, into another parse tree, suitable for describing a French sentence. In general, the syntactic transformation is the operation that maps from one tree structure to another.

The main idea behind Transfer based Machine Translation is that input (source language) sentence can be transformed in to output (target language) sentence by carrying out the simplest possible parsing structure of source language in to equivalent target language parse structure, for creating this source sentence parse tree and convert it to target language parse tree structure its required grammar rules of both source and target language. After forming the parse structure of target sentence word in the parse tree structure is searched for its meaning into bilingual dictionary.

Steps involve in translation
1. Tokenization is breaking down text into lexemes a unit of morphological analysis. Here we consider the spaces between two words for tokenization.
2. Apply morphological analysis on words to apply segmentation. In English sentence it rarely required
3. By applying the rules of English grammar assign an appropriate category to words like (noun, verb, noun phrase, adjective, adverb etc.)
4. Generate a parse tree using grammar rules of the source language.
5. Create a parse tree structure of target language using grammar rules and order of words in the target language.
6. Find the translation of all English words into Sanskrit dictionary.
7. Forms a meaningful statement.

For example
A man eats vegetables.
Narah shaakam khaadati.
Step1: Tokenization: separate the words in English sentence if there is a space between two words.
A man eats vegetables.
Token 1 Token2 Token3 Token4
Step2: Apply morphological analysis

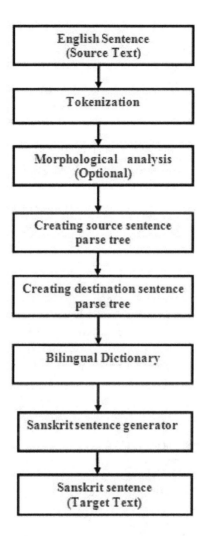

Fig. 3.3 Phases involved in Machine Translation.

Considering lexical database if there is any compound word is present then apply segmentation and if necessary separate the word. In this example, there is no any compound word.

Step3: After tokenization and morphological analysis actual words are available then tag them using rules of grammar of source language.

Here

Token1: A   : - Determiner.

Token2: man: - Subject.

Token 3: eats: - Verb.
Token4: Vegetable: - Object.

Step4: Create a parse tree of source statement using a parser.

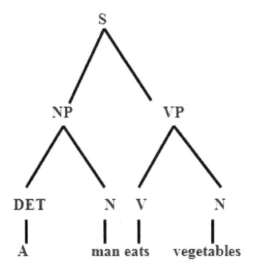

Fig. 3.4 Source sentence parse tree generation.

Step5: Creation of Equivalent parse tree in the target language using grammar rules of the target language and parse tree of the source language.

Step6: After parsing check meaning of each leaf nodes of the parse tree in a bilingual dictionary. If meaning is available to retrieve it otherwise gives errors message "meaning not available translation is not possible". If all meanings are available to target sentence will be formed by replacing the word of the leaf node of the target language parse tree and result into target sentence in Sanskrit language.

Destination sentence : - Narah shaakam khadati

A man   : - Narah   : Subject.
Shaakam   : - Vegetables : Object
Eats   : - Khaadati   : Verb

3.3 SUMMARY

This chapter has given the technical details about system overview of proposed English to Sanskrit Machine Translation system by combining Tokenization, Tagging and Parse tree generations procedure.

CHAPTER 4. ENGLISH TO SANSKRIT TRANSLATION

4.1 INTRODUCTION

In this chapter, Translator development life cycle and analysis of it is described. The development of this Translator tool is done by using the waterfall model, which suggests a systematic, sequential approach to software development that begins with customer specification of requirements and progresses through planning modeling, construction, and deployment.

Before the project begins, an estimate of project work must be done in terms of resources and time required to finish the project. Estimation of the project should be updated as the project progresses. Estimation provides all details, project planning activities that are required for the success of the project.

4.2 TASK AT EACH PHASE

4.2.1 SOFTWARE REQUIREMENT ANALYSIS

In this phase, a survey of available applications used for translations is done. Their functionality is listed. Different approaches used for translation in that translation is studied. After this survey, I found that there are different approaches to translation [Refer 3.1] from these approaches considering the requirement of this project I selected transfer-based approach for translation.
In this phase software, requirement specification document was prepared as given below.

- Scope

The goal of this work is to accept the sentence in the English language from a user and translate the sentence into the Sanskrit language without changing the meaning of the sentence.

- Objective

The objective of SRS is to ensure that all functional requirements for the project captured and clearly understood.

- Current Requirements

1. Accepting source sentence from the user.
2. Sentence Tokenization and Tagging by applying rules of grammar.
3. Generation of Parse tree in source language structure.

4. Reordering of parse tree into target language structure.

5. Preparation of database (bilingual dictionary which required for translation)

6. Replacing the leaf node (Source language word) by Target language word by searching into the database.

- **Future Scope**

This system can be enhanced to perform translation of large size text. Sanskrit can act as an intermediate language for other Indian languages, using this base multilingual translator can be possible.

- **Specific Requirement**

This sub-section describes the requirements related to the core functionality of English to Sanskrit machine translator.

- **Functional Requirements**

The system should be able to accept the sentence in simple sentence form or in compound sentences form. Tokenization of sentence should available separately. Parsing of the sentence should available separately. Translation of sentence should available in the separate window. New data addition future should be available. Font and style option for source and destination text should be available.

- **Performance requirements**

The system should provide the target text without changing the meaning of the original text. The accuracy of translation should be higher. Tokenization and parsing should be properly performed. If the meaning of a word is not available error message should be displayed.

- **Operational requirements**

Operational requirements of Tokenization algorithm: It is expected that the sentence provided to tokenizer should be a simple sentence with proper spacing and termination.

- **Operational requirements of the Parsing algorithm**

List of tokens submitted to parser with proper tagging is necessary. Rules of grammar should be available for parsing.

- **Operational requirements of the Translation algorithm**

Meaning of all words should be available in the bilingual dictionary.

- **Database requirements**

The database should be maintained using MySQL. It contains a table for source and target language vocabulary. The database should be a flexible addition of new vocabulary should be easy.

After analysis, use case models were prepared which gave the user's view of the system.

4.2.2 DESIGN

The design process creates a representation or model of the software. For this, parameters like a flow of the data, the sequence of activities to carry out a certain task were decided and with the help of that information different UML diagrams were created. The data structure for the project implementation was decided. Database and GUI designing was done. Also, test cases were decided.

4.2.3 IMPLEMENTATION / CODING

Code generation translates the design into machine readable form. Selection of language for coding, tools selection takes place. Implementation of different modules comes under the project. Implementation of GUI so that user can easily interact with translator application. Integration of all modules to interconnect different modules and system was made ready to run.

4.2.4 TESTING

Unit testing was carried out as and when small modules were completed. Then group wise they were integrated and proper working of the integrated module was tested. Finally, the whole system was tested to check whether its working is according to the requirement.

4.2.5 SUPPORT AND MAINTENANCE

Software support/maintenance reapplies each of the preceding phases to an existing program rather than a new one.

4.3 SUMMARY

This chapter has given detail about SDLC model used for project development. Task decided at each phase of the waterfall model. It also provides SRS document under software requirement analysis.

Chapter 5.
DESIGN SPECIFICATION OF ENGLISH TO SANSKRIT TRANSLATION

5.1 INTRODUCTION

For effective design following fundamental concepts are strongly considered in the design of this Translator Tool.

Abstraction—data, procedure, control abstraction

Refinement—elaboration of detail for all abstractions

Modularity—compartmentalization of data and function (optimum modularity is preferred)

Architecture—overall structure of the software

Procedure—the algorithms that achieve the function

Hiding—controlled interfaces

This chapter focuses on data flow diagram for English to Sanskrit Machine translation using NLP in detail. The purpose of this design document is to provide a comprehensive architectural overview of the system, Design considerations, and UML diagrams and to capture and convey the significant architectural decisions, which have been made on the system.

The main scope of English to Sanskrit Machine Translation system is to translate the sentence in the English language into Sanskrit sentence if the translation is not available nearest matching is available. Context based matching of words also provided if required.

- Overall system design is given by bubble chart.
- Detailed system design by focusing on DFD level 1 & DFD level 2
- Algorithms
- Logical View by class diagram
- Process View

5.2 DATA FLOW DIAGRAMS

Data flow diagrams represent the flow of input data from the input end to the output end. A data flow diagram is a pictorial representation of a system or portion of the system. It consists of data flows, processes, external entity, data store – all described through the use of easily understood symbols. An entire system can be described from the viewpoint of the data it processes with only four symbols.

5.2.1 DFD level 0

The DFD level 0 gives the overall system information. It is drawn by considering only one process. The input to the system and output generated from the system is shown in the following phase. The input to the system is English sentence and output from the system is Sanskrit sentence. Here in DFD level 0, we can come across the inputs and outputs. To generate the output, the input is undergoing different transformation and transaction.

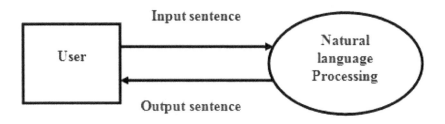

Fig 5.1 DFD Level 0

5.2.2 DFD level 1

The DFD level 1 is an expansion of single process shown in DFD level 0 generally a minimum 1:5 expansion ratio is preferred. Here in this DFD level 1, the main process is divided into the following sub processes.

1. Accepting sentence in English.
2. Tokenization of sentence.
3. Part of speech tagging.
4. Forming source language parse tree.
5. Converting source sentence parse tree into the target structure.
6. Retrieving the meaning of the words from the dictionary

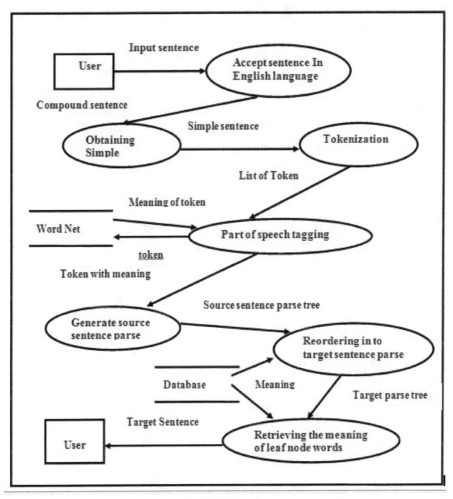

Fig 5.2 DFD Level 1

5.2.3 DFD level 2

DFD level 2 is prepared by identifying the expandable processes from DFD level 1. The general expansion ratio is 1:3. Following steps shows DFD level 2 for different modules of the proposed system.

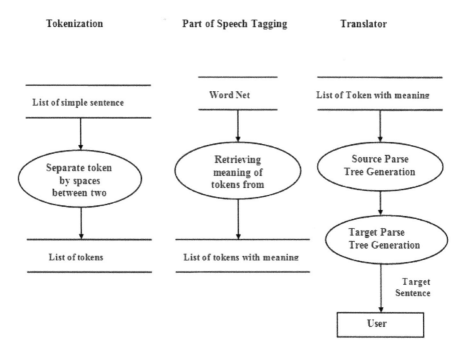

Fig 5.3 DFD level 2 for Submodules in Translation

5.3 UML DIAGRAMS

5.3.1 Class Diagram

The class diagram is given below shows classes and the relationship between them.

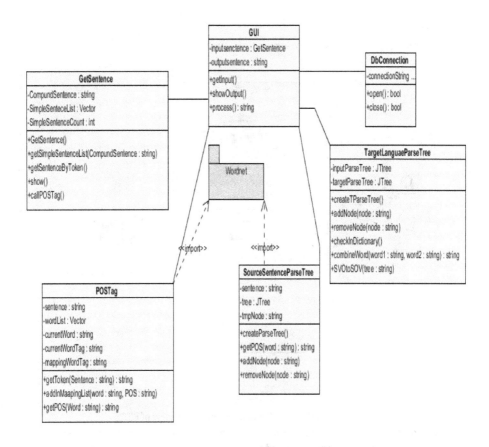

Fig 5.4 Class Diagram for English to Sanskrit Machine Translation System

5.3.2 Use Case Diagram

Use Case Diagram for Generalize view of the EST System: This diagram lists out the functionality/operation of the system as of use cases. It shows different actors which are participating in the utilization of the system.

Use Cases:

1.   **Get Sentence:** - It provides functionality for entering source text.

2.   **Get Simple Sentence:** - user may enter compound sentence it converts compound sentence into simple sentence.

3.   **Natural Language Processing:** - using concept of NLP source sentence in English language is translated in to Sanskrit language.

4.   **Sanskrit sentence:** - Displaying target sentence in separate window.

Actors:

User: - User of the system. Use the system for translation.

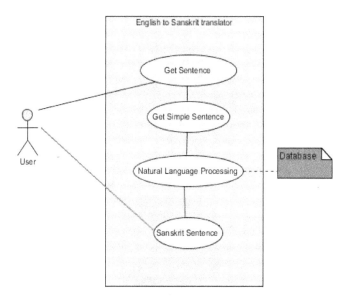

Fig. 5.5 Use case diagram for Generalize view of EST.

Use case diagram for Adding vocabulary into database:

This diagram shows the use cases required for add word into the database.

1. Get English word: - Provide functionality for entering English word.

2. Get Sanskrit word: - Provide functionality for entering Sanskrit word.

3. Save to database: - It saves the entered words into a database.

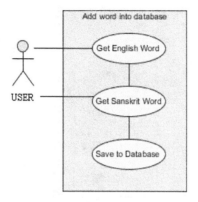

Fig. 5.6 Use case diagram for Add word to databases.

Use case diagram for NLP process:
These diagram shows include use cases of NLP use case as below
1. Tokenization: - This use case provides functionality for token generation from a sentence which entered by the user.
2. Get POS: - This use case retrieves part of speech for each token.
3. Source language parse tree: - Generate a tree of source text using grammar rules of the source language.
4. Target language parse tree: - Generate a tree of Target text using grammar rules of the target language.

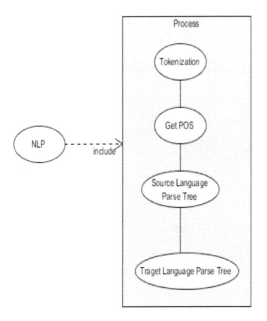

Fig 5.7 Use case Diagram for a detail view of NLP.

5.3.3 Sequence Diagram

A sequence diagram is an interaction diagram that emphasizes the time ordering of messages. The rectangle representing object involves in the translation process. The interaction between objects is shown by messages.

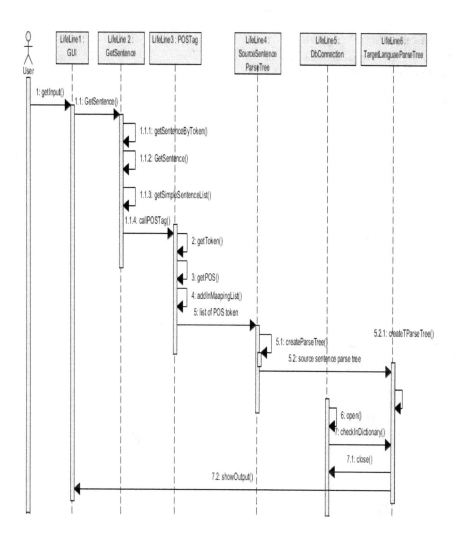

Fig 5.8 Sequence Diagram for English to Sanskrit machine translation System

5.3.4 Component Diagram

A component diagram shows the various components in the system and dependencies among a set of components.

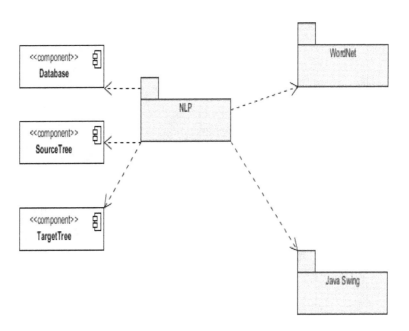

Fig 5.9 Component Diagram for English to Sanskrit machine translation System

5.3.5 Activity Diagram

It captures the flow from one behavior or activity, to the next. They are similar in concepts to a classic flowchart. Here activity diagram for translation is shown, object instances involved in translation shown by a rectangle.

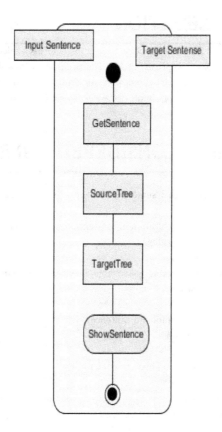

Fig 5.10 Activity Diagram for English to Sanskrit machine translation System

5.4 SUMMARY

This chapter gives the detailed design of the system using DFD and UML diagrams.

Chapter 6.
IMPLEMENTATION OF
ENGLISH TO SANSKRIT TRANSLATION

6.1 PROBLEM DEFINITION

After studying all the existing methods for machine translation, approach selected for implementing problem solution is Transfer based approach of MT. The problem is formulated to translate the English sentence into equivalent Sanskrit sentence by combining the Tokenization, Part of speech tagging, parse tree generator, and forming simple sentences from compound sentences procedure.

6.2 REQUIREMENT CONSIDERED FOR EST

1) System is used for translation of English sentences into Sanskrit sentences.

2) There are separate modules for tokenization of the sentence, using that if the user wants only tokenization of English sentence with tagging is available.

3) Similarly, a separate module for parsing is available which provide source language sentence parse tree and target language parse tree.

4) The application can be useful for compound sentences with the same efficiency   as a single sentence. Partition of sentences is possible.

5) Context based translation cases are handled using the project.

6) If we want to add a new word which is not present in the dictionary that the facility is available for the user of the application.

7) The project is user friendly if direct matching is not available nearest matching provided.

6.3 FEASIBILITY STUDY

6.3.1 Objective

To decide Whether the project can be done practically. Whether the final product will benefit its intended users.

Possible alternatives
Categories of the Feasibility Study can be divided as
1.   Economic Feasibility
2.   Technical Feasibility
3.   Operational Feasibility

6.3.2 Economic Feasibility

The most important feasibility for any business application is the economic feasibility, which is an evaluation of the development cost against the income or benefits derived from the project. This system is economically feasible since this system cost is very less.

6.3.3 Technical Feasibility

Technical feasibility was the biggest requirement analysis for English to Sanskrit MT system.
1.   As net bean is used for development, coding time is reduced by a large amount.
2.   Transfer based approach is used for Translation.
3.   The user can able to add a new vocabulary of the source and destination languages.
4.   Wordnet is used for part of speech identification for tokens.
5.   Font and Style options are provided in the GUI.
6.   Database for translation is a bilingual dictionary of source word to target word meaning. Dictionary is maintained in the MySQL database.

6.3.4 Operational Feasibility

*   User friendliness
*   Less Technical Risk: Technology (Net beans JAVA) that we are using is very powerful to implement the project
*   Proper planning and scheduling of project.
*   Implementing the project in modules and then combined it for final execution. So, avoiding exhaust coding.

6.4 RESOURCES

The next project-planning task is an estimation of the resources required for the success of the system development effort. Availability of the resource must be established at the earliest practicable time.

Hardware/Software Tools

1) Hardware
System specification (Recommended)
Pentium IV Computer with 512 MB RAM

2) Software
The software requirements for the project are as follows:
1. Windows XP
2. JAVA Net bean.
3. WordNet.
4. MySQL.

6.5 ALGORITHMS USED FOR TRANSFER BASED APPROACH

This approach is already discussed in detail in chapter 2. In this chapter, we will discuss the actual implementation of translation processes using transfer based approach and algorithm required for same.

Algorithms are divided into following part:
Source language parse tree
Algorithm1-> Simple sentence
Algorithm2 -> Parts of speech
Algorithm3 -> Parse Tree
Target language parse tree
Algorithm 4-> Convert to the target language
Algorithm5 -> SVO to SOV
Final Output
Algorithm6-> Destination Sentence

Algorithm 1:
- **Generation of Simple Sentence:** sentence entered by the user may be of any type, means simple sentence or compound sentence. In the case of a compound sentence, it contains multiple

small sentences in it. Using this algorithm, we are trying to separate each simple sentence from the compound sentence and forming the list of such sentence.

- **The need of this Algorithm:** as the processing of a simple sentence is easier than a compound sentence. We are creating a parse tree of source sentence it will become simple if the sentence is in a simple form.

- **Working of Algorithm:** accepting the sentence from the user. The sentence should not be null and its length should not be equal to zero if any one of the true sentences is an invalid sentence for translation. After that it calling the function **getsentenceByToken()** function which separates the sentence by a comma, dot, and, or.

```
1.      Input: sentence
2.      Output: List of simple sentence
3.      Vector list;
4.      if sentence is not null
5.          if sentence length ! = 0
6.          list = getSentenceByToken() // Break sentence by comma, dot,and,
or
7.      else
8.              Invalid Sentence
9.      else
10.          Invalid Sentence
11.      return list;
```

```
1.      getSentenceByToken()
2.      Input: Compound Sentence
3.      Output: Sentence Token list
4.      Tokens = Break sentence by delaminateor (", . and or")//String Tokeniz
er
5.      Vector list;
6.      for each (Temp in Tokens)
7.      {
8.          if (Temp length > 0)
9.              list.add(Temp)
10.     }
11.     return List;
```
Algorithm 2:

- **Part of Speech Tagging:** generated simple sentence acts as input for this algorithm. Tokenization and tagging these are important processes of this algorithm. The first step in this algorithm is tokenization, the sentence is split into token by considering spaces between the two words. For each token part of speech is retrieved from the word net. Finally, we will get a list of tokens and its POS.

- **Need of this Algorithm:** order of tokens in the parse tree depends on its meaning (part of speech) present in language i.e. whether it is a verb, adverb, adjective, object, subject, noun etc.

- **Working of Algorithm:** for each token in the sentence we calling function **getPOS()** which will provide the POS from Word Net. After getting POS, Token and its POS are added in to list. Finally, we will get all tokens with its POS in list form.

```
1.      Input: Simple Sentence
2.      Output: Key Value Pairs // Key Word and Value = POS (Parts of speech)

3.      Dictionary list
4.      for each (Temp in Sentence)
5.      {
6.          String pos = getPOS(Temp); //Get POS from Word Net
7.          list.add (   Temp, pos);
8.      }
9.      return list;
```

Algorithm 3:

• **Generation of Source Language Parse Tree:** an input for the algorithm is a list of tokens and its POS. nodes are added in to parse tree considering grammar rules of the corresponding language. Priority of tokens is decided by its part of speech. Associativity is also considered for the addition of token in to parse tree.

• **The need of Algorithm:** a sentence is easily represented using parse tree. Parse tree also represents the structural ordering of language which is fixed for every sentence in that language. If data is represented in the form of any data structure processing of data become easier. Here the tree is a data structure which makes sentence processing easy for translation.

• **Working of Algorithm:** This algorithm accepts the list of a token with its POS as an input and generates the Parse tree structure of source language using the algorithm or steps given in algorithm 2.

```
1.      Input: List of tokens with POS of each token.
2.      Output: Source language Parse tree.
3.      Sentence
4.          Subject
5.          Pronoun
6.          Temp2
7.              Verb
8.                  Aux Verb
9.                  Main Verb
10.         Adverb
11.         Adjective
12.         Preposition
13.         Object
```

1.   Get Sentence
2.   Add root node
3.   Get Subject and add as a first child node in the root node
4.   Check for aux verb -> Temp1
5.   Check for Verb -> Temp2
6.   Add Temp1 Temp2 as a child node in the root node
7.   Get adverb to add as a child in a root node
8.   Get Adjective add as a child in a root node
9.   Get Preposition to add as a child in a root node
10.   Get Object to add as a child in a root node

Algorithm 4:

- **Generation of target language parse tree:** source language parse tree is converted into target language parse tree.

- **A need of Algorithm:** In case of translation output is sentenced in a target language. For achieving this we required parse tree of the target language to specify the order of words in the sentence of a target language.

- **Working of Algorithm:** In this algorithm, the input is given as source sentence parse tree. This parse tree structure rearranged into target language parse tree structured using the grammar of target language.

```
1.      Input: Source language Parse Tree.
2.      Output: Target Language Parse Tree.
3.      Incremental match
4.      Check for all word
5.      N = sentence size
6.      ADD ROOT NODE
7.      While (n > 0)
8.      {
9.          Get all n word
10.         Check in dictionary
11.         if match found
12.     get target words AND ADD AS CHILD NODE IN ROOT NODE
13.     if(n== sentence size)
14.     break;
15.     make n=n-1 group
16.     }
17.     return tree;
```

Algorithm 5:

• **Changing order of sentence:** this algorithm is used for changing the order of sentence from SVO to SOV.

• **Need of This algorithm:** Order of subject object and verb in target sentence is arranged using rules of grammar of target language.

```
1.      Input: Target language tree
2.      Output: SVO to SOV
3.      Traverse tree
4.      For each (node in tree)
5.      If Node. Type == Object
6.          Remove from its place
7.          Add new node before verb node and assign object node
8.      Return tree;
```

Algorithm 6:

Get a sentence from a tree.

Show the output in target language.

6.6 COMPARISON OF ENGLISH AND SANSKRIT GRAMMAR

English is a well-known language so we illustrate Sanskrit grammar and its salient features. The English sentence always has an order of Subject-Verb-Object, while Sanskrit sentence has a free word order. A free order language is a natural language which does not lead to any absurdity or ambiguity, thereby maintaining a grammatical and semantic meaning for every sentence obtained by the change in the ordering of the words in the original sentence. For example, the order of English sentence (ES) and its equivalent translation in Sanskrit sentence (SS) is given as below.

ES: Ram   reads   book.

(Subject) (Verb) (Object)

SS: Raamah pustakam pathati.

(Subject) (Object)   (Verb);

Or

Pustakam raamah pathati.

(Object) (Subject) (Verb);

Or

Pathati pustakam raamah

(Verb) (Object) (Subject)

Thus, Sanskrit sentence can be written using SVO, SOV and VOS order.

A. Alphabet

The alphabet, in which Sanskrit is written, is called Devanagari. The English language has twenty-six characters in its alphabet while Sanskrit has forty-two characters or *varanas* in its alphabet.

B. Vowels

The English have five vowels (a, e, i, o and u) and twenty-one consonants while Sanskrit have nine vowels or *swaras* (a, aa, i, ii, u, uu, re, ree and le) and thirty-three consonants or *vyanjanas*. These express nearly every gradation of sound and every letter stands for a particular and invariable sound. The nine-primary vowel consists of five simple vowels viz. a, i, u, re and le. The vowels are divided into two groups; short vowels: a, i, u, re and le and long vowels: aa, ii, uu, ree, lee, e, ai, o and au. Thus, the vowels are usually given as thirteen. Each of these vowels may be again of two kinds: *anunasik* or nasalized and *ananunasik* or without a nasal sound. Vowels are also further discriminated into *udanta* or acute, *anudanta* or grave and *swarit* or circumflex. *Udanta* is that which proceeds from the upper part of the vocal organs. *Anudanta* is that which proceeds from their lower part while *Swarit* arises out of a mixture of these two.

C. Consonant

The consonants are divided into *sparsa* or mutes (those involving a complete closure or contact and not an approximate one of the organs of pronunciation), *antasuna* or intermediate (the semivowels) and *ilshman* or sibilants. The Consonants are represented by thirty-three syllabic signs with five classes arranged as below. *(a) Mutes: (1) Kavarga: k, kh, g, gh, nn. (2) Chavarga: ca, ch, j, jh, ni. (3) Tavarga: t, th, d, dh, ne (4) Tavarga: t, th, d, dh, n. (5) Pavarga: p, ph, b, bh, m. (b) Semivowels: y, r, l, v. (c) Sibilants: ss, sh, s* the first two letters of the five classes and the sibilants are called surds or hard consonants. The rest are called sonants or soft consonants. In Sanskrit, there are two nasal sounds: the one called *anuswara* and the other called *anunasika*. A sort of hard breathing is known as *visarga*. It is denoted by a sepcial sign: *a swara* or vowel is that which can be pronounced without the help of any other letter. A *vyanjana* or consonant is that which is pronounced with the help of a vowel. *B. Noun* According to Paninian grammar, declension or the inflections of the nouns, substantive and adjectives are derived using well defined principles and rules. The crude form of a noun (any declinable word) not yet inflected is technically called a *pratipadikai.* C. *Gender* Any noun has three genders: masculine, feminine, and neuter; three numbers: singular, dual, and plural. The singular number denotes one, the dual two and the plural three or more. The English language has two numbers: singular and plural, where singular denotes one and plural denotes two or more. There exist eight classifications in each number (grammar cases): nominative, vocative, accusative, instrumental, dative, ablative, genitive and locative. These express nearly all the relations between the words in a sentence, which in English are expressed using prepositions. Noun has various forms: *akAranta, AkAranta, ikAranta, IkAranta, nkAranta* and *makAranta.* Each of these *kaarakas*, have different inflections arising from which gender they correspond to. Thus, *akAranta* has different masculine and neuter declensions, *AkAranta* has masculine and feminine declensions, *ikAranta* has masculine, feminine and neuter declensions and *IkAranta* has masculine and feminine forms.

D. Pronoun

According to Paninian Grammar and investigations of M. R. Kale, Sanskrit has 35 pronouns. These pronouns have been classified into nine classes. Each of these pronouns has different classes as personal, demonstrative, relative, interrogative, reflexive, indefinitive, correlative, reciprocal and possessive. Each of these pronouns has different inflectional forms arising from different declensions of the masculine and the feminine form.

E. Adverb

Adverbs are either primitive or derived from noun, pronouns or numerals.

F. Particle

The particles are either used as expletives or intensive. In Sanskrit, particles do not possess any inflectional suffix, for example, *trata saa pathati.* Here, the word *trata* is a particle which has no suffix, yet the word *trata* implies the meaning of the seventh inflection.

G. Verb

There are two kinds of verbs in Sanskrit: primitive and derivative. There are six tenses (*Kaalaa*) and four moods Vimal Mishra, R. B. Mishra (*Arthaa*). The tenses are as present, aorist, imperfect, perfect, first future, and second future. The moods are as imperative, potential, benedictive and conditional. The ten tenses and moods are technically called the ten *Lakaras* in Sanskrit grammar.

H. Voice

There are three voices: the active voice, the passive voice and the impersonal construction. Each verb in Sanskrit, whether it is primitive or derivative, may be conjugated in the ten tenses and moods. Transitive verbs are conjugated in the active and passive voices and intransitive verbs in the active and the impersonal form. In each tense and mood, there are three numbers: singular, dual and plural with three persons in each.

6.7 Comparative View of English and Sanskrit

Comparative study of English and Sanskrit language.

Basic	English	Sanskrit
Alphabet	26 characters	42 characters
Number of vowel	Five vowels	Nine vowels
Number of consonant	Twenty-one consonant	Thirty-three consonant
Number	Two: singular and Plural	Three: singular, dual and plural
Sentence Order	SVO (Subject-Verb-Object)	Free word order
Tenses	Three: present, past and future	Six: present, aorist, Imperfect, perfect. 1st future and 2nd future
Verb Mood	Five: indicative, imperative, interrogative, conditional and subjunctive	Four: imperative, potential, benedictive and conditional

Table 6.1 Comparative study of English and Sanskrit language.

6.8 SUMMARY

This chapter gives the details about algorithms used for implementation of the project. Feasibility of implementation is studied. Comparative study of English and Sanskrit language which required for translation is studied.

CHAPTER 7. TESTING FOR ENGLISH TO SANSKRIT APPLICATION

7.1 INTRODUCTION

Here I tried to find out the error in the application using software testing methodology.

This document explained all strategies, testing methods and test cases I used for testing the application. I considered three types of testing for my project namely Unit testing, Integration testing and System testing from different types of testing available.

7.2 TEST PLAN FOR PROJECT

The test plan is used to describe all testing that is to be accomplished, together with the resources and schedule necessary for completion of testing on the project.

Test plan also provides background information about the application tested, test objective and risks & specific tests to be performed.

The scope of Software Test Plan (STP) is to document the testing plan of English to Sanskrit machine translation project. It involves Functional testing as well as Integration testing and Unit testing.

7.3 TESTING OBJECTIVE

Once the code has been generated, program testing begins. The testing process focuses on the logical internals of the software, ensuring that all statements have been tested, and on the functional externals; that is conducting tests to uncover errors and ensure that defined input will produce actual results that agree with required results. Testing strategies have the following generic characteristics

- Testing begins at the component level and works "outward" toward the integration of the entire computer-based system.
- Different testing techniques are appropriate at different points in time.
- Testing is conducted by the developer of the software and (for large projects) independent test group.
- Testing and debugging are different activities, but debugging must be accommodated in any testing strategy.

7.4 TESTING STRATEGY

7.4.1 Testing Process

The testing process followed for English to Sanskrit machine translation project is explained here.

1) Identify the requirements to be tested. All test cases are derived using the current Design Specification.

2) Identify the expected results for each test.

3) Identify the testing-related equipment and reference document that are required to execute the testing Process. Setup the test environment.

Test Design

i. Prepare the test cases.

ii. Prepare the test setup.

iii. Review and approve test cases.

5. Test Execution

i. Execute test cases and updates the actual results in test cases.

6. Test Report

    Create a test report for each build.

    Prepare a test summary report.

7.4.2 Build Process

The following is the Build Process to be followed for the **English to Sanskrit machine translation using NLP.** Manual testing is proved to be very effective in this case. In this approach, there is flexibility to test each and every module in detail.

As the application is made up of different sub modules like sentence partitioning, tokenization, part of speech tagging, parse tree generator and sentence translator. Several testing's we can apply on the application.

-   Testing of each module individually for functionality.
-   Test the main module which integrates the entire module.
-   Now compile the main file and generate executable.
-   Run executable and recognize the output of translator.
-   Writing the test cases manually to get the test result.

7.4.3 Types of Testing

The different types of testing that may be carried out in the project are as follows

1.   Unit Testing

2.   Integration Testing

3.   System Testing.

4.   Regression Testing

5. Black Box Testing

6. GUI Testing

Each type of testing is done using the Manual testing approach.

Sr. No.	Module	What User Sees	User Input	Expected Result	Comment
1.	Simple sentence generation	Simple English sentence	Compound sentences in English	list of simple sentences in English	Passed
2	Tokenizer	List of tokens.	Simple sentence	List of token	Passed
3	Part of speech tagging	List of tokens with meanings	List of Token	List of tokens with its meanings	Passed.
4	Source sentence parse tree generation.	Graphical form of source sentence parse tree	Vector list of tokens with meanings	Parse tree structure of source language sentence.	Passed

5	Target sentence parse tree formation	Graphical form of target sentence parse tree	Parse tree structure of source language sentence.	Parse tree structure of the target sentence.	Passed
6	Translator	Sentence in Sanskrit language	Parse tree structure for target sentence.	The translated sentence in the Sanskrit language	Passed
7	Addition of vocabulary into dictionary.	Updated database	English and Sanskrit word	Updated database	Passed

7.5 TEST CASES AND TEST RESULTS FOR VARIOUS TESTING

7.5.1 UNIT TESTING

In this project each module I consider as a unit. Use of this testing here to check that each module is working properly. Finding and fixing the error if module not giving correct output.

Table 7.1 Unit Testing Test cases.

7.5.2 INTEGRATION TESTING

A good approach to integration is to integrate two modules and check them for their functionality. In this project output of one module is act as input for another module.

Table 7.2 Integration Testing Test cases.

Sr. No	Prerequisite	Test Case Description	Steps and Data	Expected Result	Actual Result	Pass /Fail
1.	Simple sentence generation and tokenization module should be ready.	This test case used for checking whether simple sentence are received to tokenization or not	1.Give input as compound snetence . 2.click on tokenizatio n option.	List of token should be generated for all simple sentence	List of tokens generated	Pass
2	Part of speech tagging and source sentence parse tree generation module should be ready	This test case used for checking integration of POS and Parse tree module.	1.List of token is input to pos. 2.pos generate list of token with its POS . 3.It given as input to parse tree generator.	Graphicle form of source sentence parse tree should be generated	Parse tree appears in output window.	Pass
3	Target sentence parse tree structure. And translator module should be ready.	This test case used for checking the translation is properly coming or not.	1. Source sentence parse tree as input.	Provide sentence in Sanskrit language.	Obtained Sanskrit sentence in output window.	Pass

7.5.3 SYSTEM TESTING

The goal of this testing here to ensure that the system performs translation according to its requirements. System test evaluates both functional behavior and quality requirements such as reliability, usability, performance and security of application.

There are several types of system tests. The types are as follows:
• Performance testing
• Functional testing
• Load testing
• Configuration testing
• Security testing
• Recovery testing

Here I considered Load testing, Functional testing and Configuration testing.

7.5.3.1 Load Testing: load testing is carried out to check system response in the form of time for different number of statement as an input.

SR . No.	Number of input sentence at time	Expected output	Time required for Translation in Second	Actual output
1	Run with 5 simple sentence	Run Properly	44	Run properly
2	Run with 10 simple sentence	Run properly	80	Run properly
3	Run with 20 simple sentence	Run properly	110	Run properly

Table 7.3 Load Testing Test cases.

7.5.3.2 Functional Testing: It is black box in nature focus is on input and proper output for each function. Here I considered legal and illegal inputs for translation function.

Sr. No.	Test case Name	Input Sentence	Test Case description	Expected Output	Actual Output
1	Simple sentence translation	Raj is beautiful	This test case is used to check application for simple sentence. How application response and provide output.	राज सौन्दर्यम् बा	राज सौन्दर्यम् बा
2	Compound sentence translation	Raj is going to school. House is beautiful. Raj knows English, he speaks very well.	This test case is used to check application for compound sentence.	राज विद्यालयः गछ गृहम् सौन्दर्यम् बा राज आङ्ग्लभाषा सः अत्यन्तः कूपः व	राज विद्यालयः गछत् गृहम् सौन्दर्यम् बा राज आङ्ग्लभाषा जानाति सः अत्यन्तः कूपः बदति
3	English sentence with numeric data	Raj knows 100.	This test case is used to check application for sentence mix with numeric data.	राज 100 जानाति	राज 100 जानाति
4	Incomplete sentence in English.	1.School is 2. Raj knows	This test case is used to check output of incomplete sentence.	विद्यालयः बा राज जानाति	विद्यालयः बा राज जानाति
5	No input	Keep input text box blank	This test case is used to check system response if	Blank screen	Blank screen

			input is not provided.		
6	Special charac ter in senten ce.	Raj is + beautiful.	This test case is used to check application for special symbols in sentence.	No output	No output
7	Incorr ect spell words in the senten ce.	Ram house is beautiful.	This test case is used to check the response of the system with incorrect spell words in sentence	No output	No output

Table 7.4 Functional Testing Test cases.

7.5.3.3 CONFIGURATION TESTING:

In this interaction of application with different hardware and software configuration is checked.

Sr. No.	Test case Description	Software /hardware interchanged	Expected output	Actual Output
1	Check application for operating system compatibility.	1. Run application on Windows XP. 2. Run application on Windows NT. 3. Run application on Windows Vista	It has to run properly. It has to run properly. It has to run properly.	Run properly.
2	Check application for Processor compatibility.	1. Run application on Pc with Pentium 4 processor. 2. Run application on Pc with Dual core processor. 3. Run application on Pc with Core2Duo processor.	It has to run properly. It has to run properly. It has to run properly.	Run properly.
3	Check application for RAM compatibility.	1. Run application on Pc with 256MB RAM. 2. Run application on Pc with 512MB RAM. 3. Run application on Pc with 1GB RAM.	It has to run properly. It has to run properly. It has to run properly.	Run properly.
4	Check application with different Java versions.	1.Run application with jdk 1.6 2.Run application with jdk 1.7	It has to run properly. It has to run properly.	Run properly.

Table 7.5 Configuration Testing Test cases.

7.6 SUMMARY

This chapter gives the test cases for Unit testing, Integration Testing and System testing which I decided for the project.

CHAPTER 8
RESULTS AND SCREEN SHOTS

8.1 INTRODUCTION

The purpose of this document is to give results for English to Sanskrit machine translation System. Results obtained after each stage and final output is given along with screen shot.

8.2 MAIN WINDOW FOR EST APPLICATION

It shows the main window of the application, which contains the menu bar with options file, Modules and Help.

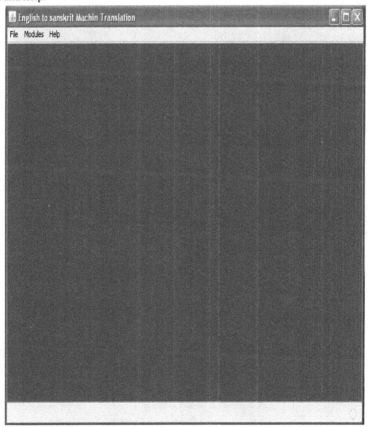

Fig 8.1 Main window for application.

8.3 Adding New Word

It provides facility for adding new words in to dictionary database.

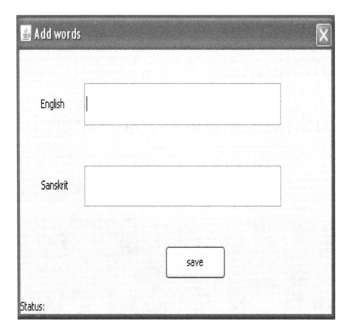

Fig 8.2 Add Word window.

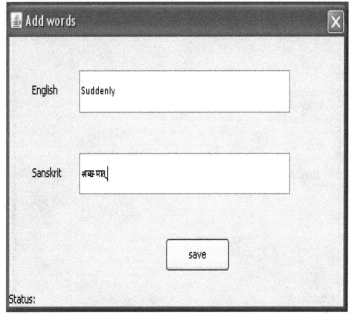

Fig 8.3 Words are entered for adding in to database.

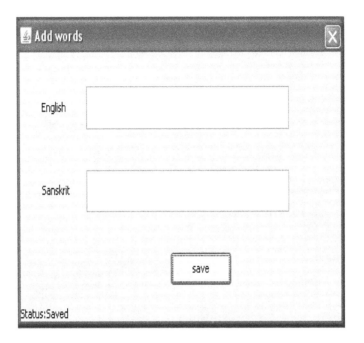

Fig 8.4 Words are successfully saved in to database.

8.4 NLP OPERATIONS

It includes options for processing English sentence and obtaining Sanskrit sentence from that by natural language processing.

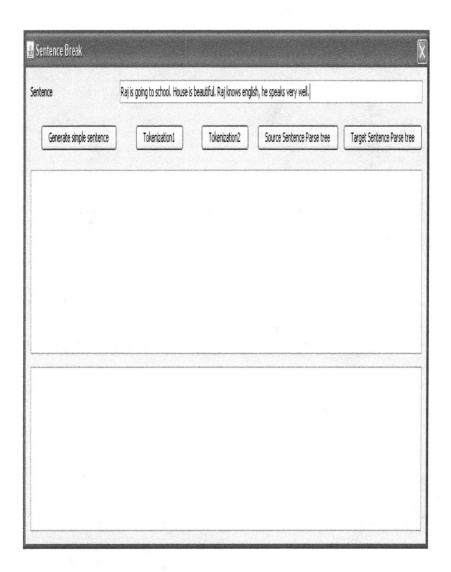

Fig 8.5 Main GUI for NLP Operations.

8.5 SIMPLE SENTENCE GENERATION

This screen shows result for Generate simple sentence button. Input for this operation is compound sentence in English and output is simple sentences.

Fig 8.6 Simple Sentence Generation

8.6 Result of Sentence Tokenization

This screen shows result of tokenization process for sentence house is beautiful.

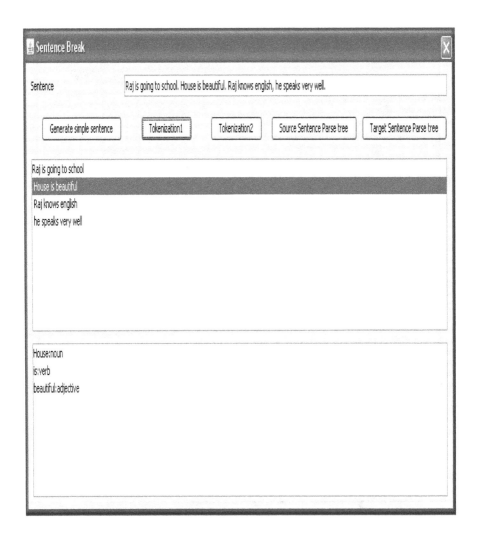

Fig. 8.7 Tokenization of Sentence

8.7 GENERATION OF SOURCE SENTENCE PARSE TREE

This screen shows the result of source sentence parse tree generation command button. Parse tree for each simple sentence is generated.

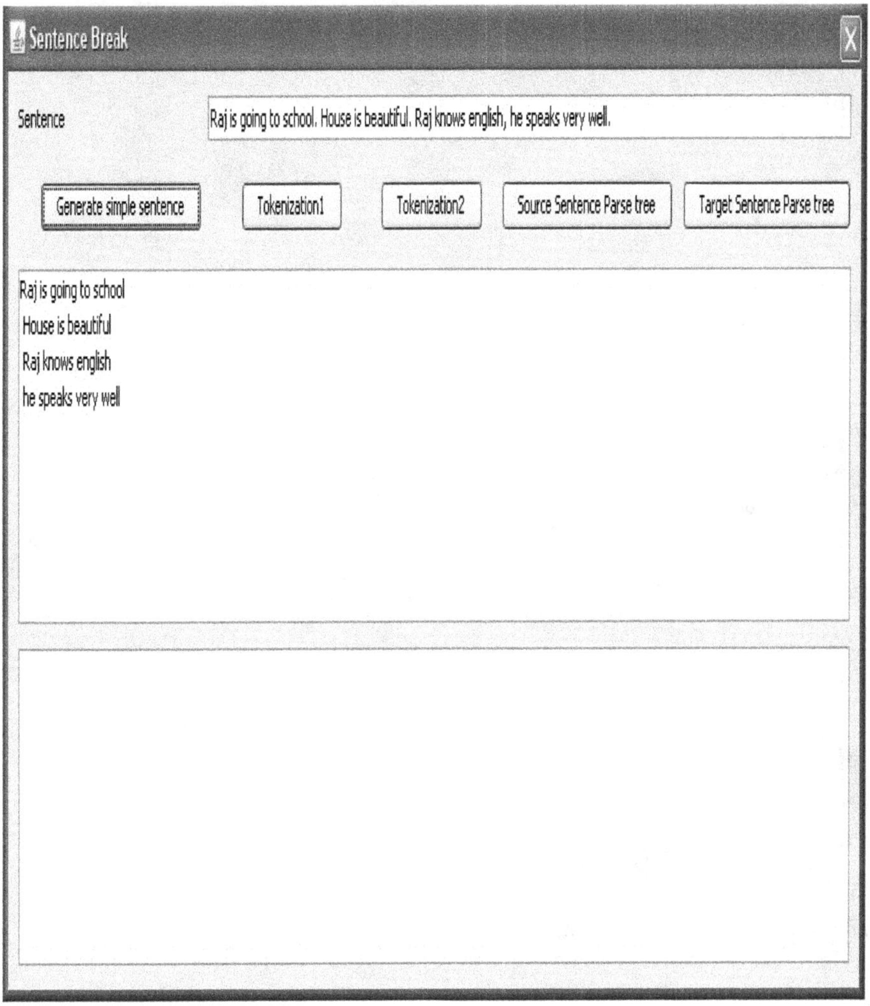

Sentence Break					X
Sentence	Raj is going to school. House is beautiful. Raj knows english, he speaks very well.				
Generate simple sentence	Tokenization1	Tokenization2	Source Sentence Parse tree	Target Sentence Parse tree	

Raj is going to school
House is beautiful
Raj knows english
he speaks very well

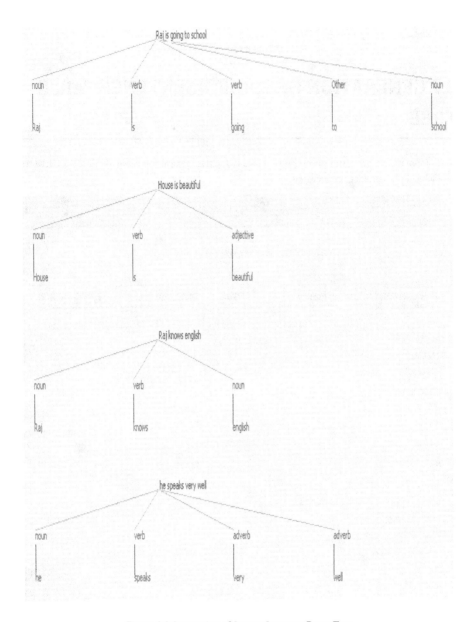

Figure 8.8 Generation of Source Sentence Parse Tree

8.8 Combining Tokens with Same POS

This screen shows the parse tree with combining tokens with same part of speech tag.

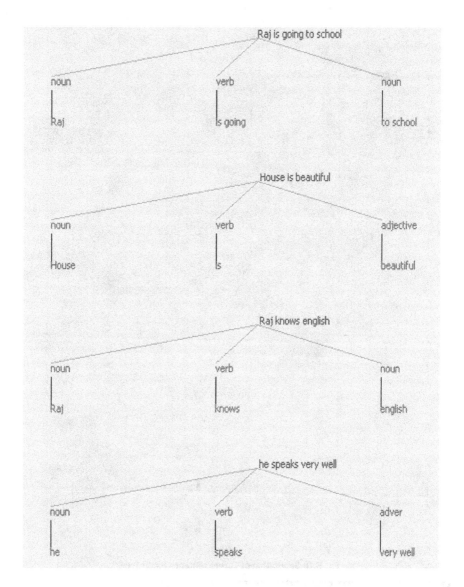

Fig 8.9 Combining words whose POS is same.

8.9 GENERATION OF TARGET SENTENCE PARSE TREE

This screen shows result of target sentence parse tree generation.

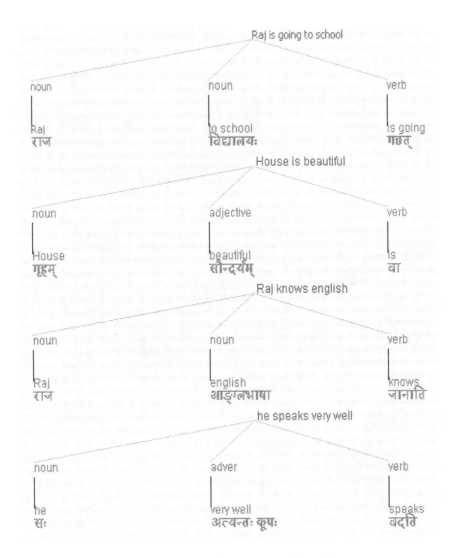

Fig. 8.10 Generation of Target sentence Parse Tree

8.10 TARGET SENTENCES IN SANSKRIT LANGUAGE

Screen shows final output of English to Sanskrit machine translation that is English written sentences are translated in to Sanskrit language.

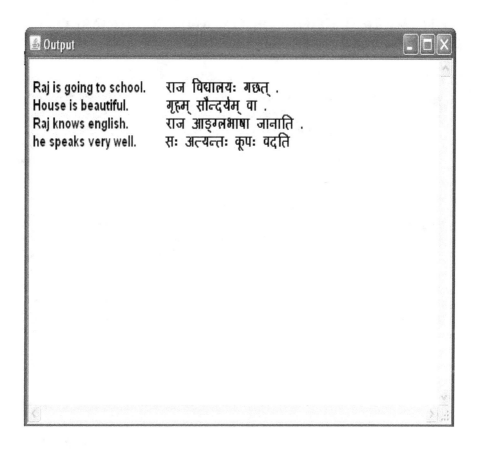

Fig. 8.11 Final out put of Translation.

CHAPTER 9. CONCLUSION AND FUTURE SCOPE

Computer based English to Sanskrit translator is successfully implemented using the natural language processing. It's followed the Transfer method comes under rule-based approach of Machine translation. This project will very useful for sharing the worldwide knowledge with Indian. Rule based approach is more superior than dictionary based approach. In dictionary based approach source text directly checked in to the dictionary for meaning. Rule based approach is not translating the sentence word by word but it also considers the POS, Grammar, context based translation and idioms of the words in sentence.

Accuracy of the project can be improved. Currently project is used for the two languages English and Sanskrit; it can be modified in to multilingual considering Sanskrit as intermediate language. Most of the Indian languages derived from the Sanskrit languages due to this Sanskrit can be used as intermediate language for translation. Now project is unidirectional that is English sentence is converted in to Sanskrit but not vice versa we can able to modify it as bidirectional.

Currently project is able to translate compound sentence; capacity of project can improve for translation of one passage or one page at a time.

REFERENCES

[1] Veda Varidhi Ramanujam, P. 1992. Computer Processing of Sanskrit (**CPAL-2 proceedings of the second regional workshop**, March 1992, IIT-Kanpur, ed. R.M.K. Sinha. pp 159-168)

[2] Aparna Subramanian, "Sanskrit to English Translator "(Dissertation submitted at Master In Computer Science, at Devi Ahilya Vishwavidyalaya, Indore)

[3] R.M.K.Shina chief Investigar IIT,Kanpur "An English to hindi Machine – Aided Translation System " (Paper presented at IEEE International conference on System, Man and Cybernetics,vancouver,canada).

[4] Vimal Mishra and R.B. Mishra, "Study of example based English to Sanskrit Machine Translation"

[5] Aasish Pappu and Ratna Sanyal," Vaakkriti: Sanskrit Tokenizer"IIIT, Allahabad (U.P.) India.

[6] Paisarn Charoenpornsawat, Virach Sornlertlamvanich and Thatsanee Charoenporn," Improving Translation Quality of Rule-based Machine Translation",Information Research and Development Division National Electronics and Computer Technology Center.

[7] Hemant Derbari, "Computer Assisted Translation System-An Indian perspective", Applied Artificial Intelligence Group center for development of advance computing, Pune.

[8] Sandip Naskar, Sivaji Bandyopadhyay,"Use of machine translation in India: Current Status "

[9] John Hutchins, "Trends in Machine Translation Research", University of East Anglia, Norwich, England.

[10] Vimal Mishra and R.B.Mishra," Divergence patterns between English and Sanskrit Machine Translation", Institute of Technology, Banaras Hindu University, (IT-BHU), Varanasi-221005, U.P, India.

BOOKS

[1] Daniel Jurafsky, James H. Martin, "Speech and Language Processing".

[2] Allen J. "Natural Language Understanding".

[3] "Introductory Guide for Machine Translator".